D1745404

Dad, I WANT TO Hear Your Story®

A FATHER'S GUIDED JOURNAL
TO SHARE HIS LIFE & HIS LOVE

"ANYONE CAN
BE A FATHER,
BUT IT TAKES
SOMEONE SPECIAL
TO BE A DAD."

– AUTHOR UNKNOWN

THIS BOOK HOLDS THE STORY OF

"Life can only be understood backwards, but it must be lived forwards."

— AUTHOR UNKNOWN

Table of Contents

Introduction

DAD, I WANT TO HEAR YOUR STORY was created to give fathers a place to chronicle and share their life stories while also inspiring meaningful conversations that strengthen family bonds.

In our busy, rapidly changing world, we often forget to pause and share our personal moments and memories with each other. What is shared, is filtered to promote reaction instead of connection.

Dad, I Want to Hear Your Story provides a gathering place for these memories. Between these pages, you will find prompts and questions that make it simple to reminisce about and remember your life.

But this book is more than just a collection of tales of the past. It's a dialogue. As fathers pen their stories, they're initiating conversations. Each memory shared is a bridge between father and family, nurturing understanding and deepening bonds.

Through these pages, children will discover their fathers as more than providers or protectors. They will meet them as dreamers, adventurers, learners—individuals with one-of-a-kind lives and a myriad of lessons to share.

To each father who chooses to embark on this journey of reflection and sharing: may this guided journal provide you with the comfort of nostalgia, the joy of reminiscence, and the power of legacy.

To each loved one who reads these stories: may you find inspiration, understanding, and pages and pages of love.

Here's to the stories that have been and the tales that have yet to be lived. With our deepest admiration for every father's journey.

"MY FATHER DIDN'T TELL ME HOW TO LIVE.

HE LIVED AND LET ME WATCH HIM DO IT."

— CLARENCE BUDINGTON KELLAND

Beginnings

What is your date of birth?

MONTH	DAY	YEAR

What time were you born?

______ : ______ a.m. | p.m.

What was your full name at birth?

Were you named after a relative or someone else of significance?

If you had been given a vote, what name would you have picked for yourself?

In what city were you born?

Were you born in a hospital? If not, where?

What was your length and weight at birth?

How old were your parents when you were born?

Did your parents have any other children before you? If so, how old were your siblings when you were born?

What were your first words?

How old were you when you started to walk?

What stories have you been told about the day you were born?

How did your parents describe what you were like when you were a baby?

What individuals cared for you the majority of the time when you
were an infant?

____

____

____

____

Was a lullaby or another song sung to help you go to sleep? If you
know any of the words, write them below.

____

____

____

____

____

____

____

____

____

____

Do you know the titles of any books that were read to you when you were a baby?

____

____

____

____

____

____

____

____

Google the following for the year you were born:

What were a few notable events that occurred that year?

____

____

____

____

____

____

Which notable movies came out that year?

____

____

____

____

What movie won the Academy Award for Best Picture?

____

____

Who won for Best Actor and Best Actress?

____

____

List a few songs that were popular.

____

____

____

____

____

What were the most popular television shows?

____

____

____

____

____

____

List the prices for the following items:

Loaf of bread: _______________________________

Gallon of milk: _______________________________

Cup of coffee: _______________________________

A dozen eggs: _______________________________

First class stamp: _____________________________

Gallon of gas: _______________________________

A movie ticket: _______________________________

The average cost of a new home: ________________

"THE TWO MOST
IMPORTANT DAYS
IN YOUR LIFE
ARE THE DAY
YOU ARE BORN
AND THE DAY YOU
FIND OUT WHY."

– MARK TWAIN

What three words or phrases best describe your childhood?

Describe what you were like when you were a kid.

Did you have a nickname when you were growing up? What was it, and how did you get it?

List the activities and sports you participated in.

What music, dance, art, or other lessons did you take? Did you enjoy them?

What were your regular chores?

Did you receive an allowance? If yes, how much was it?

When you did have money, what did you typically spend it on?

When you were a kid, what did you dream about becoming when you grew up?

Who were your best friends during your elementary school days? Are you still in contact with any of them?

What are a few movies you remember loving?

And what songs?

Television shows?

What toys do you remember being especially attached to?

What books were a big part of your childhood?

Any games you remember playing a lot?

Was there a teacher or coach from your elementary school days that had a big influence on you?

____

____

____

____

____

What did they teach you, and what was their impact?

____

____

____

____

____

____

____

____

____

____

Did you have any pets when you were growing up? If yes, what were they, and what were their names?

What is a favorite memory of a childhood pet?

What is a favorite childhood memory that fills you with nostalgia or happiness whenever it comes to mind?

If you could relive your childhood for one day, how would you choose to spend it?

____

____

____

____

____

____

____

____

"A FATHER IS
SOMEONE YOU
LOOK UP TO
NO MATTER HOW
TALL YOU GROW."

– AUTHOR UNKNOWN

Your Teenage Years

What three words or phrases come to mind when you think back on your teenage years?

____

____

____

____

Describe what you were like during this period of your life.

____

____

____

____

____

____

____

____

____

____

____

How did you dress and style your hair during your high school years?

Who were your closest friends during these years? When was the last time you spoke with any of them?

What were your parents' opinions on your choice in friends?

Was there a group or activity that your social life and friend group tended to revolve around?

How did you spend a typical weekend night during your high school years?

Was there a specific place where you and your friends would hang out after school or on the weekends?

What was your curfew?

What is a memory of a time when you missed your curfew?

How did your parents respond to your being late?

Did you date during your high school years?

If yes, what was a typical date like for you in those years?

Did you go to any school dances?

If yes, describe what they were like.

What age were you when you got your driver's license? How many times did you have to take the test to pass?

Who was the primary person who taught you to drive?

What was the make and model of the car you drove in high school?

What activities or sports did you participate in during your teens?

What did you like the most about high school?

What year did you graduate from high school?

How many students were in your graduating class?

Do you remember where you ranked academically?

What were your favorite subjects in school?

And what were your least favorite?

Were there any coming-of-age traditions that you participated in during your teens or preteens (confirmation, bar mitzvah, others)?

____

____

____

Did you ever skip school?

____

____

If yes, did you get away with it? What did you do during the time you should have been in class?

____

____

____

____

What jobs did you have during your high school years?

____

____

____

____

Do you remember how much you were paid?

____

____

____

____

What is something from high school or your teens that you would like a chance to do over?

What were a few of your favorite movies?

And television shows?

And books?

What were your favorite kinds of music?

Your favorite bands or recording artists?

What were a few of your favorite songs from these years?

If you were to give it a name, what would you say was the overall theme of your bedroom?

What color were the walls painted?

What did the bedding look like?

What did you have hanging on the walls?

Describe any additional details about how your teenage bedroom looked and felt.

Looking back on this time, which moments and experiences stand out as transformative and defining?

What advice would you give your teenage self?

What could the teenage version of you teach you today?

"IT'S NOT THE YEARS IN YOUR LIFE THAT COUNT. IT'S THE LIFE IN YOUR YEARS."

– ABRAHAM LINCOLN

What did you do after high school? Did you serve in the military, get a job, or go to college or a trade school? Something else?

____

____

____

____

What were your reasons for making this choice?

____

____

____

____

Looking back, how do you feel now about this decision?

____

____

____

____

How did this time period impact who you are today?

____

____

____

____

____

____

____

If you could go back, what, if anything, would you change about this period of your life?

____

____

____

____

____

____

If you went to college or trade school, what did you study?

____

____

____

____

Describe what you were like in your twenties.

What were your main goals and priorities during this time of your life?

What advice would you give the twentysomething version of yourself?

When you reflect on the person you were in your twenties and compare that to who you are today, what core parts of your identity or personality have stayed close to the same?

____

____

____

____

____

____

____

____

What has changed?

____

____

____

____

____

____

____

"Fathers hold their children's hands for a while but their hearts forever."

— AUTHOR UNKNOWN

Still reflecting back on your twenties, what pivotal choices or actions stand out as having had the most significant impact on the way your life moved forward?

What was your first major job after high school or college? How old were you? How much were you paid when you started?

Was there a job or profession your parents or family wanted you to pursue? What was it?

When people ask you what profession you are/were in, your response is...

How did you get into this career?

List a few of your work- and career-related achievements that you are proudest of.

Where is the first place you lived where you were the one who was responsible for paying the rent or mortgage? Do you remember the address?

How old were you when you moved there?

Did you live on your own, or did you share the place?

What was your share of the rent/mortgage each month?

How long did you live there?

What was your favorite thing about this place?

Describe the place. How many bedrooms and bathrooms did it have? What other things do you remember about it?

What is a favorite memory from your time living there?

"SOMEONE IS SITTING IN THE SHADE TODAY BECAUSE SOMEONE PLANTED A TREE A LONG TIME AGO."

– WARREN BUFFETT

Think back to when you were growing up. What are three words or phrases that best describe your family?

____

____

____

____

How many nights each week on average would your family have dinner together?

____

____

____

When you did eat together, what was the typical routine for how the meal and the time together went?

____

____

____

____

____

____

What did everyone usually talk about during the meal?

Who did most of the cooking?

And who did most of the cleanup afterwards?

When you were a kid, what were a few of your favorite things that were served for dinner?

And what were the dishes that would make you grimace?

What would happen if you wouldn't eat something?

What holiday was the biggest event for your family when you were growing up?

What were some of the most memorable ways your family would observe this holiday?

How were birthdays, anniversaries, and individual achievements commemorated by your family?

Did your family set aside regular quality time together (things like movie nights or game nights)? If so, write about what they were like.

Did you have any relatives who lived nearby who were a big part of your family life?

What role did they have in how you were raised?

What values, beliefs, and rules were strongly emphasized during your upbringing?

What were the expectations and requirements in areas such as grades, chores, and participation in extracurricular activities or sports?

In what ways does the family environment you created for your own kids compare to the one you grew up in?

Was there anything you consciously did differently?

Time can create changes in perspective. Looking back, how have your views on your upbringing and coming-of-age years changed over time?

"Life isn't about finding yourself.

Life is about creating yourself."

— GEORGE BERNARD SHAW

What is a favorite memory you have of a time you spent with your family during your childhood?

What is a favorite memory you have of a time you spent with your family as an adult?

Your Family Tree

____

MY GREAT-GRANDFATHER

(My Grandfather's Dad)

MY GREAT-GRANDMOTHER

(My Grandfather's Mom)

____

MY GREAT-GRANDFATHER

(My Grandmother's Dad)

MY GREAT-GRANDMOTHER

(My Grandmother's Mom)

____

MY GRANDFATHER

(My Dad's Dad)

MY GRANDMOTHER

(My Dad's Mom)

____

MY FATHER

MY GREAT-GRANDFATHER

(My Grandfather's Dad)

MY GREAT-GRANDMOTHER

(My Grandfather's Mom)

MY GREAT-GRANDFATHER

(My Grandmother's Dad)

MY GREAT-GRANDMOTHER

(My Grandmother's Mom)

MY GRANDFATHER

(My Mom's Dad)

MY GRANDMOTHER

(My Mom's Mom)

MY MOTHER

"WE NEVER TRULY KNOW THE LOVE OF A PARENT TILL WE BECOME PARENTS OURSELVES."

– HENRY WARD BEECHER

Parents & Grandparents

What was your mother's full name?

____

Where was she born?

____

Where did she grow up?

____

____

____

____

____

What was your father's full name?

____

Where was he born?

____

Where did he grow up?

____

____

____

____

What three words or phrases best describe your mother?

In what ways are you most like her?

Reflect on and share the qualities and values you most admire in your mother.

What three words or phrases best describe your father?

In what ways are you most like him?

Reflect on and share the qualities and values you most admire in your father.

What was your mother's maiden name?

From what part(s) of the world did your mother's family originate?

What was your father's mother's maiden name?

From what part(s) of the world did your father's family originate?

How did your parents meet?

What were their ages when they first met?

When and where were they married? How old was each at the time?

What stories have you been told about their wedding day?

List a few of their hobbies, interests, talents, and skills.

What were their educational backgrounds?

What were your parents' professions?

Did either of them serve in the military?

Parents will often repeat certain words of wisdom, sayings, and proverbs when giving advice to their kids. What are a few you often heard growing up?

Write about a favorite memory of your mother.

Write about a favorite memory of your father.

What were the names of your grandparents on your mother's side of your family?

____

____

What did you call them?

____

____

What was your maternal grandmother's maiden name?

____

Where were they born, and where did they grow up?

____

____

____

____

What was their highest level of education?

____

____

____

What were their professions?

____

____

____

"**Life is what we make it. Always has been, always will be.**"

— GRANDMA MOSES

What is a favorite memory of your grandparents on your mom's side?

Describe what they were like.

____

____

____

____

____

____

____

____

____

____

____

What were the names of your grandparents on your father's side of your family?

____

____

What did you call them?

____

____

What was your paternal grandmother's maiden name?

____

Where were they born, and where did they grow up?

What was their highest level of education?

What were their professions?

Describe what they were like.

What is a favorite memory of your grandparents on your father's side?

Did you ever meet your great-grandparents on either side of your family? If yes, what were they like?

What other individuals had a major role in helping you grow up?
What was each one's contribution to who you have become?

"YOU NEVER KNOW
HOW STRONG YOU
ARE, UNTIL BEING
STRONG IS YOUR
ONLY CHOICE."

– BOB MARLEY

Are you an only child, or do you have siblings?

____

____

Where are you in the birth order?

____

____

Do you feel things were easier or harder for you when you were

growing up because of where you fell in the birth order? Why?

____

____

____

____

____

List your siblings' names in order of their ages. Be sure to include

yourself.

____

____

____

____

____

Which of your siblings were you the closest with when you were young?

____

____

____

Which of your siblings have you been the closest with during your adult years?

____

____

____

Did you look up to any of them when you were growing up?

____

____

____

If yes, write about a time when you did something to impress them or be like them.

____

____

____

____

____

____

____

What is something you admire about each of your siblings?

Did you share a bedroom with any of them?

If yes, what are three words or phrases that best describe the experience?

What is the best part about having a sibling?

Write about a favorite memory from your childhood that shows the bond you shared with your siblings.

"THE HEART OF
A FATHER IS THE
MASTERPIECE
OF NATURE."

– PREVOST ABBE, *MANON LESCAUT*

How old were you when you first became a father?

____

Think back to the moment when you found out you were pregnant with your first child. Do you remember your first reaction or the first thing you said?

____

____

____

What were your initial thoughts, feelings, and emotions?

____

____

____

Who was the first person you told?

____

____

____

What was their reaction?

____

____

____

Write about the first time you saw your baby on a sonogram or heard their heartbeat. Be sure to include your reactions, feelings, and emotions.

____

____

____

____

____

____

____

Describe the first time you felt your baby move or kick.

____

____

____

____

____

____

____

____

What was the process for selecting your children's names?

What is the inspiration for each of your children's names?

Were there any disagreements or negotiations over any of the names?

What are a few of the standout memories of any of the pregnancies?

What were your children's lengths and weights at birth?

How old were they when they took their first steps?

What were their first words?

Is there a special song you would sing or play for your children when they were little?

What tricks would you use to help them relax or fall asleep?

Are there any specific books you remember reading to your children?

Based on all you have learned and experienced as a parent, what advice would you go back and give yourself when you were a new dad?

What was the biggest surprise about being a parent that you discovered after your first child was born?

____

____

____

____

____

____

____

____

What are the best parts about being a dad?

Write about something unexpected you have learned about yourself from becoming a father.

When you reflect on your life before and after having children, what are the significant ways becoming and being a father has changed you?

How have being a dad and raising children shaped or reshaped your perspective and understanding of your own upbringing and your parents?

"LOVE IS COMPOSED OF A SINGLE SOUL INHABITING TWO BODIES."

– ARISTOTLE

Love Firsts & Love Forevers

Do you believe in love at first sight?

Do you believe in soulmates?

What age were you when you went on your first date?

Can you remember who it was with and what you did?

How old were you when you had your first steady relationship?

Did you have any celebrity crushes when you were young? Who were the most memorable?

When you were younger, did you have a type you were attracted to? Describe it.

How did you meet our mom?

What were your first impressions of her?

Who asked out who for your first date?

____

____

____

Describe how the question was asked and the response. Where were you, and how did it happen?

____

____

____

____

____

What did you do on your first date?

____

____

____

____

What were your impressions and thoughts about her after that first date?

____

____

____

____

____

Do you remember the first time you thought that she might be "the one"? What was it about her, or what did she do to help you to feel this way?

How long did you date before you became engaged?

What is the story of your proposal?

Who was the first person you told that you were engaged?

Describe their reaction.

How much time was there between when you became engaged and the actual wedding date?

What was the process for planning the wedding like? Who did most of the work? Were there any challenges?

Did either of you have a bachelor or bachelorette party? If yes, where was it held?

Where was the wedding held?

How about the reception?

How many people were invited to the wedding?

And how many people attended?

Who were the best man and maid of honor?

And the groomsmen?

And the bridesmaids?

Any other members of the wedding party?

What was your wedding like, and who was there? Any good wedding day stories?

What moment from your entire wedding day do you remember the most vividly?

Did you have a honeymoon? If yes, where did you go?

What advice would you want to go back and give yourself the morning of your wedding day?

This is room to write about any other memories of getting married
or additional weddings you may have had.

"THE MEANING
OF LIFE IS TO
FIND YOUR GIFT.

THE PURPOSE
OF LIFE IS TO
GIVE IT AWAY."

— PABLO PICASSO

If you were to write your autobiography, what title would you select to convey and describe your life story?

____

____

____

____

What is a favorite quote, scripture, or prayer?

____

____

____

____

What superpower would you choose for yourself?

____

____

What is your biggest fear?

____

____

____

If you could live anywhere in the world for a year with all expenses paid, where would you choose?

What is a travel experience that changed your opinions and perspective about a part of the country or the larger world?

What is a favorite memory of a meal you had while traveling?

What is a favorite travel memory?

List your ten favorite destinations you have traveled to.

1. ____

____

2. ____

____

3. ____

____

4. ____

____

5. ____

____

6. ____

____

7. ____

____

8. ____

____

9. ____

____

10. ____

____

List the top ten places you would visit if money and time were no concern.

1. ______________________________

   ____

2. ______________________________

   ____

3. ______________________________

   ____

4. ______________________________

   ____

5. ______________________________

   ____

6. ______________________________

   ____

7. ______________________________

   ____

8. ______________________________

   ____

9. ______________________________

   ____

10. ______________________________

    ____

When you were growing up, what sports did you follow? Did you have any favorite teams?

Who is your favorite player of all time in any sport?

What was the first professional sporting event you attended in person?

If money was no object, what sporting event would you most want to attend?

What was the most crushing defeat you experienced playing or watching a sporting event?

____

____

____

____

What is your favorite sports movie?

____

____

____

What are a few movies from your childhood and teens that you still enjoy watching?

____

____

____

____

____

____

____

____

If you were going to make a movie about your life, what would the title be?

____

____

____

What genre would the movie be (rom-com, thriller, science fiction, drama, etc.)?

____

____

____

____

Who would you cast to play you?

____

____

How about the rest of your family?

____

____

____

____

____

____

If you had to name your ten all-time favorite can't-miss films, which ones come to mind?

1. ____

____

2. ____

____

3. ____

____

4. ____

____

5. ____

____

6. ____

____

7. ____

____

8. ____

____

9. ____

____

10. ____

____

What song would you pick as the theme song of your life?

In your opinion, which decades had the best music?

What is a song from your teens that reminds you of a special event or moment from that time? Write about that memory.

How has your taste in music changed over the years?

What is the first record (or album, cassette, CD, etc.) you can remember buying or receiving as a gift?

What was the first concert you attended? Where was it held and when? What do you remember about it?

What are the ten songs that would be on a playlist of your personal all-time favorite music?

1.

2.

3.

4.

5.

6.

7.

8.

9.

10.

What are a few television shows and movies that are a must-watch for you and your family around the holidays?

What television show from the past do you wish was still making new episodes?

How many books would you say you read each year?

When you do read, what are your favorite genres?

Who are some of your favorite authors?

What book or books have majorly impacted the way you think, work, or live your life?

What is a favorite memory from the last twelve months?

What in your life has brought you the greatest joy and contentment?

What are a few personal accomplishments you are especially proud of?

How did you define success for yourself when you were younger?

____

____

____

____

____

____

____

____

____

How do you define success for yourself now?

____

____

____

____

____

____

____

____

Which has the most impact on our lives: fate or free will?

What do you believe is the purpose of our lives?

"To do the useful thing, to say the courageous thing, to contemplate the beautiful thing: That is enough for one man's life."

— T.S. ELIOT

What role did religion have in your family when you were growing up?

____

____

____

____

____

____

____

____

Were there any specific religious rituals, celebrations, or traditions that your family observed?

____

____

____

____

____

____

____

____

How have your spiritual beliefs changed over the course of your life?

What role do prayer, meditation, or other spiritual practices play in your life?

Write about a time when your faith or your spiritual practices helped you through a challenging period.

Which individuals do you feel especially grateful to for the role they played in your life story? Be sure to describe how each one has impacted you.

When you look back over the course of your life, what events and experiences had the biggest impact in shaping the person you are today?

When you think over the ups and downs of your life, what was a time that stands out as especially demanding?

What do you do when times are challenging, and you need to find additional inner strength and perseverance?

What advice on how to live one's best life would you offer to someone in their twenties and thirties?

And what lessons about life do you think you could learn from someone in their twenties or thirties?

The following pages are for you to expand on some of your answers, share more memories, and/or write notes to your loved ones.

Hear Your Story
Books & Guided Journals

At Hear Your Story®, we have created a line of books focused on giving each of us a place to tell the unique story of who we are, where we have been, and where we are going.

Sharing and hearing the stories of the people in our life creates a closeness and understanding, ultimately strengthening our bonds.

Mom, I Want to Hear Your Story:
A Mother's Guided Journal to Share Her Life and Her Love

Dad, I Want to Hear Your Story:
A Father's Guided Journal to Share His Life and His Love

Grandmother, I Want to Hear Your Story:
A Grandmother's Guided Journal to Share Her Life and Her Love

Grandfather, I Want to Hear Your Story:
A Grandfather's Guided Journal to Share His Life and His Love

Tell Your Life Story:
The Write-Your-Own-Autobiography Guided Journal

To My Wonderful Aunt, I Want to Hear Your Story:
A Guided Journal to Share Her Life and Her Love

To My Uncle, I Want to Hear Your Story:
A Guided Journal to Share His Life and His Love

Mom & Me: Let's Learn Together Journal for Kids

Mom, I Want to Learn Your Recipes
A Keepsake Family Memory Cookbook

Grandmother, I Want to Learn Your Recipes
A Keepsake Family Memory Cookbook

Dad, I Want to Learn Your Recipes
A Keepsake Family Memory Cookbook

Grandfather, I Want to Learn Your Recipes
A Keepsake Family Memory Cookbook

Aunt, I Want to Learn Your Recipes
A Keepsake Family Memory Cookbook

Uncle, I Want to Learn Your Recipes
A Keepsake Family Memory Cookbook

Sibling, I Want to Learn Your Recipes
A Keepsake Family Memory Cookbook

Friend, I Want to Learn Your Recipes
A Keepsake Family Memory Cookbook

FIND MORE FAMILY CONNECTION AT
@hearyourstorybooks
hearyourstorybooks.com

About Hear Your Story

AT HEAR YOUR STORY®, WE'RE DEDICATED TO capturing and cherishing life's priceless moments. We passionately believe that within everyone is a treasure of memories and stories that need to be told, cherished, and passed on through generations.

Our journey began from a deeply personal heartache for our founder: watching Alzheimer's steal his father's creativity, curiosity, and memories. From that pain emerged a profound realization—the importance of preserving every precious life story.

Hear Your Story offers more than a beautifully designed journal. We provide a bridge to the past, guiding you or your loved one through cherished memories. It's a gift of reflection, connection, and legacy.

Envision you and your family sitting together as your loved one's journal is shared, smiles everywhere, conversations sparked, and connections deepened. In an age where moments can easily fade, Hear Your Story offers something tangible, lasting—a treasured heirloom of life's adventures.

Join us, and let's celebrate every tale. At Hear Your Story, we turn memories into heirlooms.

Published by Hear Your Story, an imprint of Sourcebooks
1935 Brookdale RD, Naperville, IL 60563-2773
(630) 961-3900
sourcebooks.com

Originally published as *Dad, I Want to Hear Your Story* in 2019
in the United States of America by EYP Publishing, LLC.

Printed and bound in the United States of America.
VP 10 9 8 7 6 5 4 3 2 1